PRENTICE HALL DISCOVERIES

THE UNEXPECTED

PEARSON
Prentice Hall

Boston, Massachusetts
Upper Saddle River, New Jersey

Copyright © 2007 by Pearson Education, Inc., publishing as Prentice Hall, Boston, Massachusetts 02116. All rights reserved. Printed in the United States of America. This publication is protected by copyright, and permission should be obtained from the publisher prior to any prohibited reproduction, storage in a retrieval system, or transmission in any form or by any means, electronic, mechanical, photocopying, recording, or likewise. For information regarding permission(s), write to: Rights and Permissions Department, One Lake Street, Upper Saddle River, New Jersey 07458.

Pearson Prentice Hall™ is a trademark of Pearson Education, Inc.

Pearson® is a registered trademark of Pearson plc.

Prentice Hall® is a registered trademark of Pearson Education, Inc.

ISBN-13: 978-0-13-363642-0
ISBN-10: 0-13-363642-9
4 5 6 7 8 9 10 V088 15 14 13 12 11

PRENTICE HALL DISCOVERIES

The Unexpected

Can all conflicts be resolved?

Table of Contents

Social Studies Connection:
First Bull Run: Front Row Seat to War 4

◎ *A front row seat to war makes observers aware of the depth of the conflict.*

Science Connection:
When Tsunamis Strike 22

◎ *People struggle to get over the damage and trauma left by a natural disaster.*

Humanities Connection:
The Sitcom Story 40

◎ *Sitcoms usually end up with some kind of a resolution to the conflict.*

Mathematics Connection:
Math in Motion 58

◎ *Some athletes try to defy the natural laws of motion to achieve their goals.*

Glossary 76

Imagine you heard that two great armies were going to meet in battle just miles from where you live. Some of your friends and neighbors are planning to watch the battle in real time, as it's developing. They expect it to be a grand show. Would you go, too? What do you think you'd learn from watching a war in progress?

For clues to the answer, consider the experiences of hundreds of civilians who witnessed the first major battle of the Civil War. The First Battle of Bull Run, on July 21, 1861, was fought not far from Washington, D.C. The battle is remembered as the first **victory** for the Confederacy, as a humiliating **defeat** for the Union, and for the odd presence of spectators. Yet for everyone involved—even the winners—the battle taught painful lessons about conflict, starting with the idea of what war is all about.

VOCABULARY

victory (VIK tuhr ee) *n.* the success you achieve by winning a battle, game, or race

defeat (dee FEET) *n.* the loss of a battle, game, or race

This painting shows General Stonewall Jackson commanding Confederate troops at the First Battle of Bull Run.

5

This photograph, taken by a Confederate photographer, shows damage to Ft. Sumter at the beginning of the Civil War. The Confederate flag was raised after the fort surrendered.

Just One Great Battle

To understand the significance of Bull Run, let's back up to the beginning of the Civil War. It started on April 12, 1861, when Confederate forces opened fire on Fort Sumter. The Union fort sat on an island in the harbor of Charleston, South Carolina. The shelling went on for a day and a half, though the battle was nearly bloodless. Only a horse inside the fort was killed. Charleston residents climbed to their rooftops to watch the bombardment. We can **assume** it must have seemed like some kind of exciting show with amazing fireworks.

Yet, when the fort surrendered and the shelling **ceased**, a war had actually begun. The various ways that leaders on both sides had tried for years to **mediate** and find compromises to avoid all-out war had failed. The conflict between North and South that had been fought mainly with words would now be decided in battle. Or, more precisely, in a common view of that time, in one great heroic battle!

Vocabulary

assume (uh SOOM) *v.* think that something is true, although you have no proof of it

ceased (SEEST) *v.* stopped

mediate (MEE dee ayt) *v.* try to help two people, groups, or countries stop arguing and make an agreement

Through the Looking Glass of History

When we study history, we have to remember a very important **aspect** of it: perspective. Today, we have the benefit of knowing what happened. We know that it would take four long years to reach another April day, in 1865, when the Civil War would end. By that time, some 620,000 men on both sides were dead. We can learn from thousands of books and documentaries that explain and **interpret** the people and events that influenced the course of the war.

But in mid-April of 1861, no one knew what was ahead. Both sides operated from the strong and certain **conviction** that the war would be decided with a quick victory. Men rushed to sign up. They feared the war would end before they had a chance to get into the fight. Southern soldiers enlisted for a year. Northern volunteers only had to serve for ninety days. Three months and the war would be over.

So what was this idea that war was a one-battle wonder? People in the nineteenth century were indeed guided by a belief that wars could be determined by a single great standoff. Not only were there examples from conflicts in Europe, there were military histories that spread the idea. One of the most widely read was titled *Fifteen Decisive Battles of the World from Marathon to Waterloo,* written by Sir Edward Creasy, an Englishman, and published in 1851. Creasy's book, like similar military histories, was meant for popular reading, not strategy. It tended to simplify events and boil complicated battles down to easy-to-understand conclusions. Battles were tests of great leaders and great courage. They were decided in favor of the side that was fighting for the better cause and had more claim to character and virtue.

Consequently, as Americans all around the country chose sides, they were confident their side was the "right" one. As the spring of 1861 turned into summer, both North and South were eager for the opportunity to prove the rightness of their cause—unity or independence—through a clash of their growing armies.

Vocabulary

aspect (AS pekt) *n.* the specific part that you are observing or studying

interpret (in TUR pruht) *v.* explain the meaning of; have or show one's own understanding of the meaning of

conviction (kuhn VIK shuhn) *n.* strong belief; certainty

consequently (KAHN si kwent lee) *adv.* as a result

These men joined the 2nd Rhode Island Infantry Regiment during the Civil War.

Inching Toward a Fight

By July of 1861, the action of the war had moved from South Carolina to Virginia. Washington, D.C., the Union capital, and Richmond, the Confederate capital, were only about one hundred miles apart. Both armies positioned their troops to protect their own capitals from capture. Both were preparing to **respond** to attack.

But "action" would be a stretch in describing what was really happening in the war. There were some minor battles here and there, but no large clash of men and arms. The great battle had yet to take place. In the North in particular, the push to **force** a confrontation that would decide the war became louder and stronger. "On to Richmond" was the collective call from newspaper headlines, Washington officials, and ordinary folk alike.

The clock was ticking for the Union army. With each passing day, the three-month volunteers were getting closer to going home. Many were counting the days. They had discovered there were clear **distinctions** between the idea of war and what it was actually like. Those differences included, **incredulously**, the opposite of what they might expect. War, as it turns out, can be boring! They were tired of camp life in the heat of summer. They were tired of waiting for battle.

So was their commander-in-chief. Abraham Lincoln knew there would soon be no army with which to fight. In order to keep the North determined and **resolute** that this was a conflict worth fighting, there had to be a battle. If the first group of volunteers returned home

Richmond, Virginia, was the Confederate capital during the Civil War.

with nothing to show for their three months away, Lincoln **perceived** it would be much harder to get more volunteers to take their place.

Vocabulary

respond (ri SPAHND) *v.* react to something that has been said or done

force (FOHRS) *v.* make someone do something they do not want to do

distinctions (di STINGK shuhnz) *n.* the noting of differences between things

incredulously (in KREJ oo luhs lee) *adv.* with doubt or disbelief

resolute (rez uh LOOT) *adj.* determined; resolved

perceive (puhr SEEV) *v.* grasp mentally; make note of; observe

11

Take the Army and March!

Lincoln began pushing the Union commander, General Irvin McDowell, to take the army and march. McDowell was worried. He knew his troops weren't ready for a big fight. They weren't trained as soldiers. Until three months earlier, they had been farmers and factory workers. It takes time to organize soldiers into **presentable** fighting units that are prepared to meet the enemy. McDowell did not yet have the military experts to train thousands of soldiers.

The Confederate army was actually in much the same shape. Their recruits were young men who had answered the call to raise a Southern army. Most did not own slaves. They were fighting to defend their own homes and homelands.

However, with the constant cries in the North for a march to Richmond, the Confederates were expecting an attack. At the same time that Lincoln was prodding his general to move, the Confederate commander Pierre Beauregard was **simultaneously** placing his soldiers in position to block an invasion. The stage was set for a great match at last.

General Irvin McDowell stands with his staff. McDowell was a career officer who commanded Union army troops.

Vocabulary

presentable (pree ZENT uh buhl) *adj.* in proper order for being seen or met by others

simultaneously (sy muhl TAY nee uhs lee) *adv.* at the same time

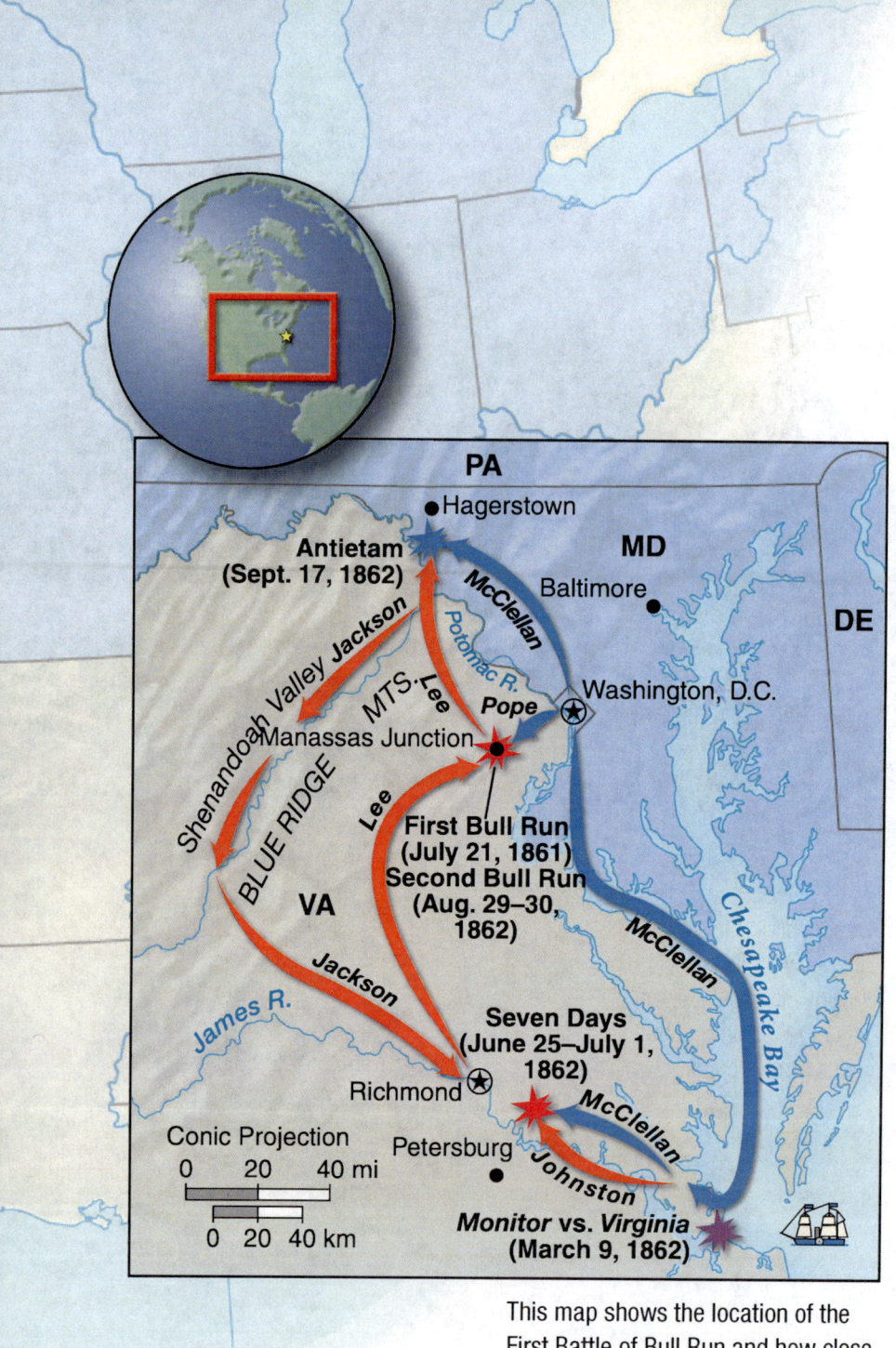

This map shows the location of the First Battle of Bull Run and how close it was to Washington, D.C.

Picking Berries on the Road to Battle

The Union army set off toward Richmond on July 16, 1861—three days before the battle at Bull Run, named for a creek that runs near Manassas, Virginia. They marched twenty-five miles. It took two and a half days—twice as long as it would later, when they were seasoned soldiers.

The atmosphere was more like a picnic than preparation for **aggression**, like a military attack. Soldiers stopped to pick blackberries and drink water in the scorching heat. "They would not keep in ranks, order as much as you please," General McDowell wrote. "They were not used to denying themselves much; they were not used to journeys on foot."

Adding to the festive air were the spectators from Washington who came out to cheer the Union army. Some accounts describe the civilians as people of great **affluence** who packed their carriages with champagne for toasting victory. Many were senators and congressmen who had pushed for the attack.

The soldiers were also excited to have an audience. "We thought it wasn't a bad idea to have the great men from Washington come out to see us thrash the Rebs," wrote a Massachusetts volunteer. **Evidently**, from these reports, it didn't occur to either the civilians or Union troops that they could actually lose.

VOCABULARY

aggression (uh GRESH uhn) *n.* angry or threatening behavior or feelings that often result in fighting
affluence (AF loo uhns) *n.* wealth; abundance
evidently (ev uh DENT lee) *adv.* obviously; clearly

This painting shows a Union supply train as it races down a road during the First Battle of Bull Run.

Battle Watchers Far and Near

The civilian spectators are one of the famous details of the First Battle of Bull Run. We know it was not **unique** to have civilians watching a battle. Charleston residents had done the same when Fort Sumter was attacked. What was different about Bull Run was the size of the battle, with thousands of troops on each side.

July 21 was a Sunday, a day off from work for most people in Washington. As news spread that the big battle was about to take place, people rode out at daybreak to watch. It's estimated about five hundred actually witnessed the fight.

What they saw varied greatly depending on where they were. A large number were on the hills outside the town of Centreville, a good five miles from the battle. They saw mainly smoke from the cannon fire and heard the crash and crackle of gunfire. Using binoculars and opera glasses, they watched the distant fight, certain that the Union forces were superior and would **dominate** the enemy. After a very loud boom, one woman quoted by a newspaper reporter spoke for the crowd: "Oh my! Is that not first-rate? I guess we will be in Richmond this time tomorrow."

Some civilians wanted a closer view of the battle. They included an Ohio judge named Daniel McCook who came to visit his son Charles, an officer with an Ohio regiment. McCook parked his carriage near where his son's men were positioned to fight. Then he invited his son to join him for lunch!

Vocabulary

unique (yoo NEEK) *adj.* the characteristics that make one thing different from others

dominate (DAHM uh nayt) *v.* rule or control by superior power or influence

17

Panic in the Ranks

Looking back, it seems as though these battle watchers and berry-picking soldiers were poking fun at war and treating it with **derision**. More likely, they were simply way too confident that they would win.

To make a long shifting day of battle short, here's what happened. At first it seemed like the Union was winning. When Charles McCook took time out to have lunch with his father, it might not have seemed like a foolish thing to do.

However, in the afternoon, events changed dramatically for the Union. More Confederate soldiers arrived to reinforce the Southern forces. Then General Beauregard ordered his men to attack. As Union soldiers watched a mass of Confederate troops **approach** their battle lines, the Northern troops panicked.

It was a **degrading** and dishonorable end to the battle for the Union army. Soldiers threw aside their weapons and ran for it. In military jargon, it was a "rout"—every man for himself. Soon the roads back toward Washington were clogged with Union soldiers fleeing for safety.

Watching Death and Defeat

And what of the civilians who had come to witness a victory? Some learned in traumatic ways that war is not just a little disagreement and minor **friction** between enemies. Charles McCook was visiting his father yet again in the afternoon when Confederate troops broke through. Judge McCook watched as his son was mortally wounded.

Charles McCook, a captain with the 2nd Ohio Volunteers in the Union Army, was killed during the First Battle of Bull Run.

Elsewhere, some dignitaries who had moved closer to the battle front now got an **acute** lesson in the very real dangers of war. New York Congressman Alfred Ely received a truly sharp one at the point of bayonets and guns. He was captured by troops from South Carolina and nearly shot. Ely spent six months as a prisoner in Richmond. Only when both sides agreed on a **negotiation** to exchange prisoners was he released.

However, evidence seems to **refute** the popular image that civilians were part of the mass retreat. Most were too far away to get tangled up with the soldiers. Their efforts to return to Washington most likely did not **aggravate** the situation or make it worse.

Vocabulary

derision (di RIZH uhn) *n.* contempt; ridicule

approach (uh PROHCH) *v.* come near or nearer to

degrading (dee GRAYD ing) *adj.* insulting, dishonorable

friction (FRIK shuhn) *n.* disagreement or angry feelings between people

acute (uh KYOOT) *adj.* sensitive; sharp

negotiation (ni goh shee AY shuhn) *n.* official discussions between two or more groups or individuals who are trying to agree on something

refute (ri FYOOT) *v.* give evidence to prove an argument or statement false

aggravate (AG ruh vayt) *v.* make someone angry or annoyed

19

The Glory and Horror of War

As Civil War history goes, First Bull Run is famous for the inexperience of the troops. However, it also introduced one of the best generals—Thomas "Stonewall" Jackson. The great Southern commander earned his nickname in the battle. During the hours when the North seemed to be winning, Jackson planted his men and stood like a "stone wall" against the oncoming Union troops. His bravery and that of his men helped turn the tide that day.

If Stonewall Jackson and his legendary daring provided the glory of battle, there was horror in far greater measure. Unlike Fort Sumter, plenty of blood was

This painting shows the important Confederate commanders during the Civil War.

shed at Bull Run. Soldiers vomited at the sight of the wounds of others. Yet this fight, with only a few thousand killed and wounded, would pale compared to the bloodshed to come.

So the big battle had been waged—and the Union had lost. But far from ending the Civil War, First Bull Run was only the beginning. The North **renounced** the idea that one battle would settle the war. Far from giving up, President Lincoln called for 500,000 more troops to serve for three years.

In time, over three million men on both sides would be part of the conflict. Countless civilians would find themselves in harm's way, but probably few ever treated battle like the viewers of Bull Run. It was lesson enough that war is not a spectator sport!

Discussion Questions

1. Compare the civilians at Bull Run being curious about watching a battle with our modern coverage of war today. What are the similarities and differences?

2. What are the lessons about conflict that you recognize from the Battle of Bull Run? Explain.

3. It is said that those who do not learn from history are condemned to repeat it. What do you think it is about human nature that people, in fact, often don't learn from history and repeat the same mistakes again and again?

Vocabulary

renounced (ri NOWNSD) *v.* gave up

WHEN TSUNAMIS STRIKE

Tsunamis are one of the most destructive forces on earth. These massive ocean waves can extend for hundreds of miles and grow to thirty or more feet in height. They have the power to destroy anything that stands in their paths: trees, animals, homes, and people. How have people learned to live with such a powerful force of nature? Read on to find out.

Tsunami: A Monster Wave

It's two o'clock in the morning in your little coastal village. Sleeping soundly, you are awakened by your mother roughly shaking your shoulder.

"Wake up and get dressed," she says. "We have to hurry."

Too sleepy to argue, you **cooperate**. Soon you and the rest of your family are hurrying along the road from your village to the hill that rises behind it.

Standing on the hill, you watch waves break on the shore in the moonlight. Miles off the coast, another wave is coming—one you can't yet see. From a boat out at sea, it might seem a little tall and fast but, from your spot in the hill, you see something different.

VOCABULARY

cooperate (koh AHP uhr ayt) *v.* act or work together with another or others for a common purpose

These photos show the December 26, 2004 tsunami as huge waves crash onto beaches in Thailand.

First, the water pulls hundreds of feet back from the shore. Then, it rushes forward as a massive wave—a wall of water taller than a building. The wave surges inland for hundreds of yards, slamming into anything and anyone in its path. You are watching a tsunami, one of the most destructive forces on earth.

A few minutes pass after the big wave hits. Just when you're starting to think it's over, another one comes. It picks up the debris from the first wave, swirls it around on shore, and pulls back out to sea. Hours pass before the big waves stop.

Tsunamis cause tremendous destruction and leave survivors homeless.

Human beings are powerless to stop a tsunami. Yet, over the years, people have learned how to live with them. We now understand how tsunamis form and how they travel across an ocean. We've also learned how to prepare for them and **change** our way of thinking about them. More recently, we've learned how to detect them when they're still out in the ocean, before they hit the shore.

How a Tsunami Forms

Earthquakes cause most tsunamis. Earthquakes don't just take place on land. They also can occur on the ocean floor, and when an underwater earthquake is big enough, it can cause a tsunami.

The plates of the earth's crust are constantly pushing against one another. When a plate slips, it causes an earthquake. When this happens on the ocean floor, the movement of the earth's crust disturbs the water above it.

Vocabulary

change (CHAYNJ) *v.* become different; make someone or something become different

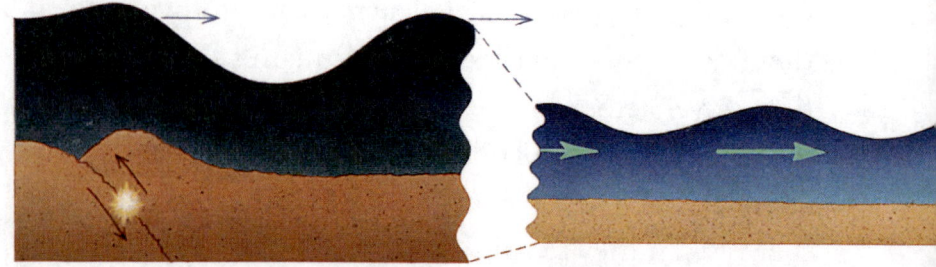

This diagram shows how a tsunami forms and how the waves change as they approach the beach.

If the earthquake is small, it makes no noticeable difference in the size of the waves, but a large earthquake can jolt the ocean's surface, causing a large wave. This is how a tsunami begins.

This first big wave soon splits into two, and each half travels off in a different direction. This means that one earthquake can cause tsunamis on opposite sides of an ocean. In deep water, the tsunami moves fast and can travel at speeds of almost 500 miles per hour. Out in mid-ocean, the tsunamis aren't especially tall. They may just be a few feet in height, but the small size of these waves **obscures** their tremendous power.

The Tsunami Strikes

As a tsunami **approaches** the shore, it slows down. As it slows, the water in the wave starts to pile up and the wave gets narrower. As a result, its height is **maximized**, so that it may tower thirty or more feet above the shore. This increase in height also pulls water back from the shore, so that the beach appears much larger than nor-

mal. This **aspect** of a tsunami presents a special danger. People may wander out onto the exposed shoreline out of curiosity. This is the exact opposite of what they should do, however.

When the tsunami comes in, the tall narrow wave **expands**, surging onto the shore. Unlike a normal wave, it doesn't end at the beach. Instead, it reaches inland for hundreds of yards uprooting trees, flooding houses, and drowning people who haven't moved to higher ground. Most tsunamis don't curve and break like regular ocean waves. Instead, they flood the land like a very big, quick-moving tide.

Vocabulary

obscure (ub SKYOOR) *v.* conceal or hide

approach (uh PROHCH) *v.* come near or nearer to

maximize (MAK suh myz) *v.* increase something as much as possible

aspect (AS pekt) *n.* the specific part that you are observing or studying

expand (ek SPAHND) *v.* become large in size, number, or amount; make something become larger

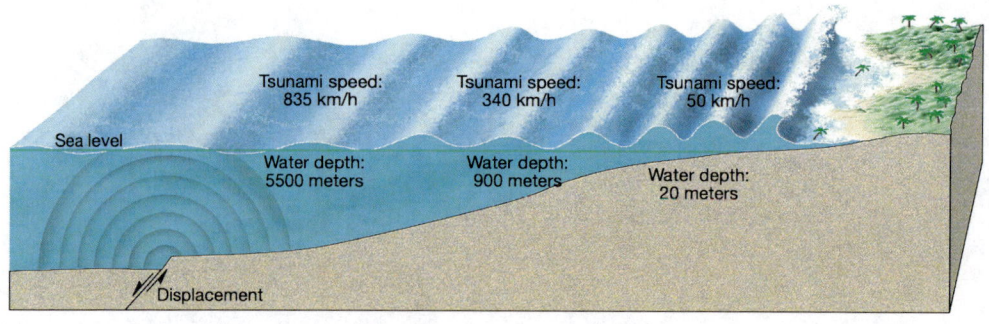

The coastline will be struck by a number of large waves caused by an undersea earthquake.

The first big wave may not be the only one. Depending on the size of the earthquake and the shape of the coastline, many more waves may strike before the tsunami **ceases**.

Learning From Tsunamis

It's known that tsunamis can travel incredible distances. In 1700, an earthquake, near the coast of what's now the state of Washington, triggered a tsunami. That wave raced across the ocean and struck Japan—more than 4,000 miles away! Records from that time tell how the tsunami destroyed homes and flooded villages.

It's not just earthquakes that cause tsunamis. In 1883, Mount Krakatoa exploded in one of the biggest volcanic eruptions in history. The eruption was so earth-shaking that it generated several tsunamis, the biggest of which was reported to be over 120 feet tall. The waves slammed into nearby islands and killed almost 40,000 people. They were so big and so powerful that they carried a metal ship almost three miles inland.

People have learned that it's important to react the right way when a tsunami strikes. On May 22, 1960, the biggest earthquake ever recorded struck near the city of Valdivia, Chile, in South America. The quake was followed by a deadly, destructive tsunami. The Chilean coast was the first place to be hit. The wave flooded coastal towns and surged up a local river. Before it struck, some people noticed that the waters were receding from the shore. They knew this **indicated** a tsunami might be coming and headed to higher ground.

VOCABULARY

ceased (SEEST) *v.* stopped
indicate (IN di kayt) *v.* show; hint at

This Japanese print from the 1700s recalls great waves that have struck the coast of Japan.

However, many others stayed put. They survived the quake only to die in the tsunami. One man even ran down to his waterfront warehouse to save his belongings after the first wave hit. **Consequently**, he was swept away along with his warehouse when the second wave came in.

A few hours after the tsunami devastated the Chilean coast, another wave struck the city of Hilo, Hawaii. The residents of Hilo had known that a tsunami might come. The city had even set off sirens as a warning, but many people didn't realize that the sirens were telling them

Nothing is left standing in Arica, Chile, after a large tsunami flattened the town.

to flee to higher ground. They thought that the sirens would be followed by orders telling them what to do. Other people fled to higher ground only to return after the first waves hit, thinking they were safe. In all, 61 people died and almost 300 were injured.

The tsunami wasn't through yet. In the early morning of May 23, it hit Japan—all the way on the other side of the Pacific Ocean. Another 138 people died there. A fireman saved the people of one village. He **perceived** that the water in the town harbor was moving strangely. **Disturbed** by what he saw, he gave the warning to move to higher ground in time to escape the tsunami.

The Indian Ocean Tsunami of 2004

The worst tsunami in history happened on December 26, 2004. The cause was an earthquake near the island of Sumatra, not far from where the Krakatoa tsunamis had hit over a hundred years before. All around the Indian Ocean, tsunamis struck. Villages in Indonesia and Sri Lanka, beach resorts in Thailand—all were flooded and destroyed. Some islands were completely washed over by the waves of the tsunami.

Vocabulary

consequently (KAHN si kwent lee) *adv.* as a result
perceive (puhr SEEV) *v.* grasp mentally; make note of; observe
disturb (di STERB) *v.* make someone feel worried or upset

Satellite photos show Banda Ache, Indonesia, before and after the December 26, 2004 tsunami struck. At least 40,000 people died in Indonesia.

32

Once again, people's lives depended on understanding the best way to **respond** to the tsunami. Some knew to run for higher ground when they saw the ocean pull back from the shore. One girl remembered a lesson about tsunamis from her geography class and warned her whole family.

In India, a man **relied** on what he had learned from watching a television show about tsunamis. He led most of the people in his village to high ground, saving their lives. There were also reports of animals fleeing from shore before the tsunami hit. In some cases, people **evidently** took the fleeing animals as a warning, and followed them to safety.

Too often, though, the tsunami caught people in the lowlands, close to the shore. All in all, the tsunami was responsible for over 200,000 deaths and a great deal of human **suffering**.

Unlike previous tsunami disasters, photos and news quickly reached people all over the world via the Internet. People felt tremendous **compassion** for the survivors. They sent money and aid to help them rebuild their lives.

Vocabulary

respond (ri SPAHND) *v.* react to something that has been said or done

rely (ree LY) *v.* trust someone or something to do what you need or expect them to do

evidently (ev uh DENT lee) *adv.* obviously; clearly

suffering (SUH fur ing) *n.* experiencing physical pain or distress

compassion (kuhm PASH uhn) *n.* strong feeling of sympathy for people who are suffering, and a desire to help them

Tsunami Warning!

If human beings had the same awareness that animals seem to have, we could flee to higher ground before a tsunami even approached the shore. Since they don't, humans have had to come up with other ways of detecting tsunamis.

The first tsunami detection system was developed in response to a tsunami that hit Hawaii in 1946. Early tsunami warning systems relied on two things. One was a seismometer, which was used to monitor earthquake activity on the ocean floor. The other was a tide gauge, which was used to measure the height of waves as they approached the shore.

However, these systems weren't very accurate. A seismometer could detect the size of an earthquake, but this just allowed people to make an educated guess about the size of the waves it generated.

Tide gauges weren't reliable, either, because the shape and depth of the shore near the gauge had such a big impact on the size of the wave. A wave that was only slightly higher than normal in one harbor could flood a town somewhere else, and even if the tide gauge for a harbor showed that a wave was a tsunami, that didn't give the people living nearby much time to evacuate.

Dr. Charles McCreery watches the computer tracking system for a tsunami on December 28, 2004 in Ewa Beach, Hawaii.

Of twenty tsunami warnings issued after 1946, fifteen wound up being false alarms. Clearly, a better system was needed.

Building a Better Tsunameter

To improve their ability to predict killer waves, scientists developed the tsunameter. The tsunameter uses a measuring tool that sits on the ocean floor, far from shore. It measures the water pressure of the ocean above it. As a wave passes overhead, the pressure increases. The bigger the wave, the bigger the increase in pressure.

The wave data is passed to a buoy that sits on the ocean's surface. The buoy beams the information to a satellite high above the earth. Scientists can then **examine** this **evidence** and figure out whether a big wave is really on its way. They can also **analyze** the shape and depths of the coastline the wave is heading

This buoy is part of a tsunami warning system being tested on Sunda Straights off the island of Java, Indonesia.

for and predict the damage it will do. Understanding this allows them to **conclude** whether it will be necessary to evacuate the people living there.

The tsunameters **earned** people's respect for the accuracy with which they could predict the behavior of these waves. Many of the devices were placed in the Pacific Ocean, where most tsunamis form.

Unfortunately, none were in place in the Indian Ocean at the time of the 2004 tsunami. Many of those deaths could have been prevented if people had been warned in advance that a tsunami was coming. Since then, work on an Indian Ocean warning system has begun, so the next tsunami that strikes the region may not be quite so deadly.

The Waves Keep Coming

Even with a warning system in place, tsunamis are incredibly dangerous. After all, there's no way to prevent a tsunami, and all people can do is get out of its way. Even the best system will give no more than a few hours' warning. In that time, people have to react quickly and get to safety.

Vocabulary

examine (eg ZAM uhn) *v.* study carefully

evidence (EV uh duhns) *n.* facts that serve as clues or proof

analyze (AN uh lyz) *v.* examine or think about something carefully in order to understand it

conclude (kuhn KLOOD) *v.* decide by reasoning

earn (ERN) *v.* get or deserve as a result of something you have done

37

To keep themselves safe, people can continue to put warning systems in places that don't have them today. People who live near the water should also remember that if an earthquake strikes, they could **infer** that a tsunami may be coming.

People can also **emphasize** tsunami preparedness. It's not enough just to know that a tsunami is on its way.

The word *tsunami* is a Japanese word that means "harbor wave."

To really save lives, any place that sits close to the ocean should have an evacuation plan to get people to safety. Some people take the attitude that it doesn't make sense to prepare for a tsunami because they'd likely die first in the earthquake that causes it. However, the experience of many earthquake survivors who have perished in tsunamis **refutes** that idea.

Human beings may have their **differences**, but they can all agree on one thing: standing in the path of a tsunami is no place to be.

Discussion Questions

1. How is a tsunami an example of conflict? What are some actions that can be taken to resolve the conflict?

2. What are some other ways that people have resolved conflict caused by natural disasters? Are there any natural disasters that can be prevented? Explain your answer.

3. How are the conflicts that have resulted from tsunamis being resolved? Use specific examples to support your answer.

VOCABULARY

infer (in FER) *v.* draw conclusions based on facts

emphasize (EM fuh syz) *v.* show that an opinion, idea, or quality is especially important; say a word or phrase louder or higher than others to give it more importance

refute (ri FYOOT) *v.* give evidence to prove an argument or statement false

differences (DIF uh uhns ez) *n.* dispute; quarrel

39

THE SITCOM STORY

Since the 1950s, families have gathered around the TV to watch their favorite sitcoms.

A lot of people turn on the TV to tune out. They sit and watch hours of "mindless" entertainment. Yet, even the simplest television comedies help us understand life. They show people facing and solving conflicts. When we watch sitcoms, we learn strategies for handling conflict—whether we want to or not.

HUMANITIES

Sitcoms have been around since the beginning of television. Half-hour comedies were popular in the 1950s. Today, people still watch their favorite sitcoms every week. However, that doesn't mean that the sitcom genre has remained the same since the early days. In fact, sitcoms have changed so much that viewers from the 50s might be baffled by today's TV comedies. The once comforting world of simple conflicts and easy resolutions has been replaced by a much more modern and complicated view of the world.

41

Sitcom Basics

Some basic terms and definitions will help to **analyze** the way sitcoms have changed over the years. These terms can apply to any sitcom, from *I Love Lucy* to *Fresh Prince of Bel-Air*.

Situation vs. Plot Sitcom stands for situation comedy. The situation is the basic setting and set-up of the program. The situation does not change from week to week. Here are some of the most common situation types:

- **Family Life:** Many sitcoms **focus** on a single family. Examples include *Leave It to Beaver, Father Knows Best, The Brady Bunch, All in the Family, Married . . . with Children, The Cosby Show, The Simpsons,* and *Malcolm in the Middle*.
- **Friends and Neighbors:** Some sitcoms **emphasize** connections between friends and neighbors, rather than a single family. Examples include *I Love Lucy, The Honeymooners, The Odd Couple, Laverne & Shirley, Three's Company, Cheers,* and *The Golden Girls*.
- **At the Office:** Other sitcoms focus on the workplace. Examples include *The Mary Tyler Moore Show, Taxi, The Office, NewsRadio,* and *30 Rock*. School sitcoms like *Saved by the Bell* also belong in this category.
- **Fish Out of Water:** Another class of sitcoms focuses on one character or group of characters placed in an unusual or uncomfortable setting. For example, *Green Acres* imagined a rich couple from New York moving to a rural countryside. In *The Beverly Hillbillies*, a rural family was transplanted from the hills of Tennessee to posh California.

The Honeymooners was a very popular sitcom during the 1950s.

- **Gimmicks:** Some sitcoms are based on a catchy gimmick. *Bewitched* placed a witch in modern suburbia. *My Favorite Martian* included one character from outer space; *Alf* used the same premise, but with a furrier alien.

The situation is not the same as the plot. The situation stays the same from week to week, but the plot each week varies. Characters face and solve new conflicts

Vocabulary

analyze (AN uh lyz) *v.* examine or think about something carefully in order to understand it

focus (FOH kuhs) *v.* concentrate on one object or idea

emphasize (EM fuh syz) *v.* show that an opinion, idea, or quality is especially important; say a word or phrase louder or higher than others to give it more importance

each week. However, when you **examine** sitcoms more closely, you start to realize that many television characters do not learn very much. They confront **similar** problems every week. Yet, they **approach** every problem as if it were brand new. Television characters seldom **acquire** wisdom from their struggles, because they have to return next week and still have the same personality.

The 24-Minute Half Hour The commercial break is an essential part of the sitcom structure. The presence of these breaks has helped to shape the evolution of the sitcom. In the early days of television, the rules for commercial breaks were not rigid. Today, a half-hour of television usually includes about 6 minutes of commercials. There are usually three commercial breaks. This diagram shows how a half-hour sitcom is traditionally structured.

Teaser	Act One	Act Two	Tag
1 to 3 minutes	9 to 10 minutes	9 to 10 minutes	1 to 3 minutes

The function of the teaser is to grab an audience's attention. Act One **identifies** and develops the main conflict and ends on a high point of tension. The commercial break relieves tension slightly. Then Act Two expands the conflict, adding new elements or complications. The conflict can be wrapped up at the end of Act Two or in the tag. The tag often ends the show with one last punch line or joke. It can also reinforce the idea that everything is resolved and the situation of the show has returned to normal.

Three Kinds of Characters Every sitcom includes three kinds of characters:

- **Main characters** are the focus of the series. They **dominate** the series and receive the most attention. In a family sitcom, the main characters are the family members. In a workplace sitcom, the main characters are usually key staff members and a boss. Main characters usually **participate** in every episode.
- **Secondary characters** do not appear every week, but do show up more than once. A secondary character might be a grandmother or neighbor that visits regularly. Secondary characters **expand** the world of a sitcom. They are often more exaggerated than the main characters. Writers often **isolate** a single strong characteristic for secondary characters, such as greedy, nosy, jealous, or stuck-up. As this list suggests, secondary characters often have more negative traits than main characters.

Vocabulary

examine (eg ZAM uhn) *v.* study carefully

similar (SIM uh luhr) *adj.* alike

approach (uh PROHCH) *v.* come near or nearer to

acquire (uh KWYR) *v.* buy or obtain something; learn or develop knowledge or skills, by your own efforts

identify (eye DEN tuh fy) *v.* recognize and correctly name someone or something

dominate (DAHM uh nayt) *v.* rule or control by superior power or influence

participate (pahr TIS uh payt) *v.* take part in an activity or event

expand (ek SPAHND) *v.* become large in size, number, or amount; make something become larger

isolate (EYE suh LAYT) *v.* set apart from others; place alone

45

- **Episode characters** are not regular members of the cast. These characters appear on just one episode (or sometimes two or three). Episode characters can include well-known guest stars. Like secondary characters, episode characters often **enhance** a show by creating conflict. Their strong personalities and **convictions** often lead to comic disagreements, most of which end with everyone **cooperating** happily at the end of the half hour.

The First Sitcom Plots

The earliest sitcoms presented fairly straightforward plots. A conflict was established in the teaser or Act One. Tension builds through Act Two. The resolution is presented at the end of Act Two or in the Tag. The entire episode focuses on just one problem.

For example, *Leave It to Beaver* was a classic family sitcom that ran from 1957 to 1963. Each week, Theodore Cleaver, whose nickname is "the Beaver," gets into trouble. By the end of the half hour, everything is OK and he learns a valuable lesson as a result. In one episode, Beaver loses his haircut money, so he decides to do the job himself. The predictably terrible results teach him to be more careful with his money. In another episode, he is afraid to tell his parents that he was dropped from the school band. In the end, he learns that he should always **communicate** honestly with his family.

These basic plots suggest that audiences do not always watch sitcoms for adventurous plots. In fact, predictability may be an attraction, rather than a cause for **derision**.

Viewers find a predictable plot comforting. In many series, plots are chosen for their universal appeal. The audience can **conclude** that people on TV are "just like them."

Another advantage of a simple plot is that it leaves more room for comedy. Writers might **select** a plot that is easily resolved in order to give the leading characters more time to simply be funny. After setting up a comic condition, they need to leave enough time for the actors to get their laughs. This is especially true of sitcoms centered around a comic star, like *I Love Lucy*.

Lucille Ball and Desi Arnaz played Lucy and Ricky Ricardo in the sitcom *I Love Lucy*. Vivian Vance and William Frawley played their neighbors, Fred and Ethel.

Vocabulary

enhance (en HANS) *v.* improve the quality or condition of

conviction (kuhn VIK shuhn) *n.* strong belief; certainty

cooperate (koh AHP uhr ayt) *v.* act or work together with another or others for a common purpose

communicate (kuh MYOO ni kayt) *v.* express your thoughts and feelings clearly, so that other people understand them

derision (di RIZH uhn) *n.* contempt; ridicule

conclude (kuhn KLOOD) *v.* decide by reasoning

select (suh LEKT) *v.* choose something or someone by carefully thinking about which is the best or most appropriate

Close Up on *I Love Lucy*

This close analysis of one *I Love Lucy* episode will show how a traditional sitcom plot develops.

Sitcom: *I Love Lucy*
Episode: "The Handcuffs"
First Aired: October 6, 1952

Series Situation: Lucy and Ricky Ricardo live in Manhattan in the same building as their friends and landlords, Ethel and Fred Mertz. Ricky is a bandleader at the Tropicana club, and Lucy often dreams of joining in on his act.

Plot:

Act 1, Scene 1: In the Ricardo's living room, Fred bores Lucy, Ricky, and Ethel with his magic tricks. He tries to impress them by escaping from a pair of handcuffs, but Lucy shows that they are fake and easily removed.

Scene 2: Lucy complains that Ricky does not spend enough time with her. As a joke, she gets Fred's trick handcuffs and handcuffs herself to Ricky while he is asleep. When he wakes up, they cannot remove the cuffs. Fred explains that Lucy took the wrong pair of handcuffs. The pair they are wearing is from the Civil War era and Fred does not have a key. They call a locksmith, who cannot come until the next day.

Scene 3: Lucy and Ricky try to go to sleep while handcuffed together. The situation offers many opportunities for slapstick, or broad physical comedy.

Act 2, Scene 1: The next morning, the locksmith arrives. He cannot open the cuffs and has to return home to get the right keys.

Scene 2: The locksmith has not returned and Ricky is late for his club act. He and Lucy go to the Tropicana.

Scene 3: Backstage, Ricky's agent says he must go on. Ricky reluctantly agrees.

Scene 4: Ricky sings a song while Lucy stands behind a curtain. Because he cannot use his right hand, Lucy places her hand through the curtain. She's in on the act, even if it's just her right arm. Finally, as the song ends, the locksmith arrives and removes the handcuffs.

Analysis: The conflict is simple and easily resolved. The fun of the episode lies in Lucy and Ricky's comic reactions to the situation.

The Plots Thicken

Sitcom plots stayed with a single focus for many years. These simple plot structures could be **adapted** to fit almost any situation. They work for everything from the down-home humor of *The Andy Griffith Show* to the alien-meets-girl weirdness of *Mork and Mindy*. In the 1970s, shows like *All in the Family* and *Maude* began to tackle tough social problems, like racism and sexism. But it was another 1970s show, *M*A*S*H,* that launched a new direction in sitcom story structure.

VOCABULARY

adapt (uh DAPT) *v.* change something so that it can be used in a different way or for a different purpose

The sitcom *Scrubs* focuses on the professional and personal lives of several characters working at Sacred Heart Hospital, a fictional teaching hospital.

*M*A*S*H* was one of the first sitcoms to focus on more than one plotline in a single episode. Each episode usually had two plots, one broadly comic, the other more serious. Since then, many other sitcoms have broadened their plot structure.

Today, multiple plot threads **enrich** many sitcoms. *Seinfeld* was a hugely popular show with four main characters: Jerry, Elaine, George, and Kramer. Many episodes juggled four different plots, one for each character. Other series in which you might **perceive** more than one plot include *Scrubs, That 70's Show, Frasier,* and *The Simpsons.*

Close Up on *M*A*S*H*

This plot analysis will help you **appreciate** the **distinctions** between a traditional sitcom, like *I Love Lucy,* and one with multiple plot threads.

Sitcom: *M*A*S*H*

Episode: "Mail Call Three" (This was the third *M★A★S★H* episode to focus on mail.)

First Aired: February 6, 1978

Series Situation: The personnel of a Mobile Army Surgical Hospital are stationed behind enemy lines during the Korean War.

Plot:
Act 1, Scene 1: Mail arrives after a three-week delay.

Scene 2: Radar delivers the mail. Benjamin Pierce mistakenly receives letters written to another soldier with his name. He reads the love letters aloud. The letters are the focus of derision. B.J. Honnicutt gets a letter from his wife and becomes deeply homesick.

Scene 3: Radar is upset because his mother wrote to say that she has a new boyfriend. Klinger enters, angry because he has discovered that his wife wants a divorce. She is in love with another man. Klinger asks Colonel Blake for leave to go home.

Scene 4: People watch a comedy in the movie tent. However, Radar and B.J. concentrate, **respectively**, on mother and wife. Klinger is also upset and demands to

Vocabulary

enrich (en RICH) *v.* improve the quality of something, especially by adding things to it

perceive (puhr SEEV) *v.* grasp mentally; make note of; observe

appreciate (uh PREE shee ayt) *v.* recognize and be grateful for; think well of; understand and enjoy

distinctions (di STINGK shuhnz) *n.* the noting of differences between things

respectively (ri SPEK tiv lee) *adv.* in the order previously named

The cast of *M*A*S*H* is shown during the filming of an episode.

go home. Everyone assumes that Klinger's reaction is another one of his tricks to leave the war, but Klinger insists that his wife has broken his heart.

Act 2, Scene 1: Klinger again asks Colonel Blake for leave to go home. The colonel says Klinger can make a phone call but not go home.

Scene 2: B.J. is increasingly homesick. Klinger tells Father Mulcahy that he is planning to run away from the army, known as going AWOL ("absent without leave"). Father Mulcahy advises him not to.

Scene 3: Radar asks for Pierce's advice. Radar cannot accept that his mother has a boyfriend. Pierce says that Radar is being unfairly jealous and admits that he once kept his father from remarrying and now regrets it.

Scene 4: B.J. wakes up Radar in the middle of the night to make a phone call home.

Scene 5: Father Mulcahy reports to Colonel Blake that Klinger has gone AWOL.

Scene 6: Honnicutt talks to his wife in San Francisco. She reassures him that she still loves and needs him.

Scene 7: The other Captain Pierce shows up to get his mail. Pierce must admit that he read the other man's mail.

Scene 8: Klinger returns to the camp.

Scene 9: Klinger explains to Colonel Blake that he was about to leave when he realized that if his wife left him for another man, she does not deserve him. He decided it was not worth getting in trouble for going AWOL.

Tag: The men toast to Klinger as things return to normal.

Analysis: Four conflicts are developed and resolved: Pierce reading someone else's mail, Radar's discomfort with his mother's boyfriend, B.J.'s homesickness, Klinger's feelings about his wife. The episode emphasizes believable conflicts rather than broad comedy.

The Camera Connection

There are two main ways that sitcoms are filmed. The method of filming can affect the plot structure.

Multiple-camera Setup Some sitcoms use several cameras at the same time. Each episode is filmed in front of a live studio audience. The results are then edited. This system was first used regularly by *I Love Lucy*. Two outer cameras focus on the lead characters. They take close-ups. The other cameras take a wider view of the entire set.

This system is inexpensive and efficient. Lighting remains the same for all shots. Editing takes less time. The multiple-camera setup lends itself well to plots that are simple and focus on one main conflict.

After *I Love Lucy,* many sitcoms and soap operas began to use the multiple-camera setup. Family-based shows like *The Cosby Show, The Nanny,* and *Everybody Loves Raymond* often used this setup.

Single-camera Setup This system uses just one camera. Series that use one camera very often do not use a live studio audience. Scenes can be filmed out of order. Lighting can be changed from shot to shot.

The distinctions between the two systems are often apparent in the final product. Viewers may perceive that the finished product from a single-camera setup looks more polished. The single-camera method is more like a movie. Plots can be more complicated, with several settings per act. Sitcoms that use single camera setups include *Gilligan's Island, The Brady Bunch, Malcolm in the Middle, Curb Your Enthusiasm, Scrubs,* and *My Name Is Earl.*

Sitcom Plus Suds

Friends was a hugely popular sitcom that ran from 1994 to 2004. The series revolved around six close friends who live in Manhattan: Ross, Monica, Chandler, Joey, Phoebe, and Rachel. Like many modern sitcoms, episodes often included more than one plot. Each character might be involved in a different conflict each week.

One of the innovations of *Friends,* however, was that it combined elements of sitcoms with the structure of a soap opera. In addition to episode conflicts, there were also longer story lines that reflected changing relationships among the friends. The friends dated, sometimes married, divorced, and yet still remained friends. Un-

Joey, Chandler, Rachel, and Monica are shown in a scene from *Friends*.

like most sitcoms, in which the situation remains the same week after week, the situation was always slightly changing.

Friends also used a popular technique from dramatic television: the season-ending cliffhanger. At the end of the third season, Ross had to decide between Rachel and another woman. Viewers were left to wait until the next season to see whom he would select.

Close Up on *Seinfeld*

Seinfeld was often described as a show about "nothing." This classic episode shows how a very simple plot structure can be surprising.

Sitcom: *Seinfeld*

Episode: "The Chinese Restaurant"

Elaine, Jerry, and George are shown in a scene from *Seinfeld*.

First Aired: May 23, 1991

Series Situation: Jerry Seinfeld lives in Manhattan with his friends Elaine and George.

Plot:

Act 1, Scene 1: Jerry, Elaine, and George go to a Chinese restaurant before a movie. They have to wait for a table. Elaine is very hungry. George waits for a pay phone to be free so he can call someone. They are told the table will be ready in five or ten minutes.

Act 2, Scene 1: They are still waiting. Elaine tries to bribe their way to a table. Finally, they are all discouraged and decide to leave. As soon as they leave, their table is ready.

Analysis: The episode takes place in real-time. The conflict is humorously ordinary. Although the network was originally against airing an episode with so little conventional plot, it became one of the most popular episodes. Viewers may **interpret** the episode as a commentary on the daily conflicts of modern life.

Discussion Questions

1. What is your favorite sitcom? How are its plots usually structured? What kinds of conflicts does it present?

2. Do you think that people can learn by watching television? Why or why not?

3. Some observers believe that multiple plot threads are better for us because they help us develop strong critical thinking skills. Do you agree? How do you support your opinion?

4. What sitcoms would you recommend for young viewers? What lessons about conflict resolution might they learn by watching episodes from these programs?

5. How are sitcoms similar to and different from dramatic television series? Do they use similar plot structures? Do characters respond to conflicts differently on a dramatic series than on a sitcom?

Vocabulary

interpret (in TUR pruht) *v.* explain the meaning of; have or show one's own understanding of the meaning of

MATH IN MOTION

There she goes! The snowboarder starts slowly, then plunges down the steep icy walls of the half-pipe. At the lip of the other side, she rockets up into the air into a looping spin called an alley-oop. She follows that with an eye-popping series of rolls, flips, corkscrew twists, and turns. Back and forth she goes, up and down. Each trick seems to take more **dexterity** than the last. As an observer, you have only one question: "How does she do it?"

Would you believe that every move a snowboarder makes is an expression of mathematics in action? Is it possible that every twist and turn, every whirl and flip is the result of a conflict between **forces**? To find out more about these forces and how they affect your actions, read on!

To perform even the simplest snowboard trick, you need three things: a snowboard, snow, and a hill. *Slope* is the measure of how steep your hill is. In general, the steeper the slope, the faster you go.

In the diagram, snowboarder 1, for example, is on a flat slope. So, it's unlikely she'll go anywhere without a push of some kind. Snowboarder 2, on the other hand, will zoom down what is called a *negative* slope. Snowboarder 3 will glide on an uphill, or positive, slope.

Vocabulary

dexterity (deks TER uh tee) *n.* skill using the hands or body
force (FOHRS) *n.* a push or pull on an object

If this "slope talk" all seems confusing, just remember: A positive slope is uphill. A negative slope is downhill. To test yourself, try identifying the slope for each of the snowboarders shown. Is it positive, negative, or flat? Then **differentiate** a steep slope from a moderate one. Finally, match each snowboarder to location A, B, C, D, or E on the half-pipe, or U-shaped snowboarding course. Pay attention to the starting position.

A Closer Look at Slope

Mathematically speaking, slope is just the ratio of *vertical* to *horizontal*. You can write slope in terms of *x* and *y* values using symbols that look like triangles called *deltas*. Delta means "change in."

$$\text{slope} = \frac{\text{change in vertical}}{\text{change in horizontal}} = \frac{\text{change in } y}{\text{change in } x} = \frac{\Delta y}{\Delta x}$$

Let's **obtain** a slope for our uphill snowboarder. As shown in the diagram, the slope rises 4 units for every

4 units that it moves to the right. In math terms, this translates to Δy/Δx = +4/+4. Simplified, we get a slope of +1.

Compare this measurement to the slope of the downhill snowboarder in the second diagram. Now the y-value goes down 1 unit for every unit it moves to the right. So Δy/Δx = -4/+4, or -1.

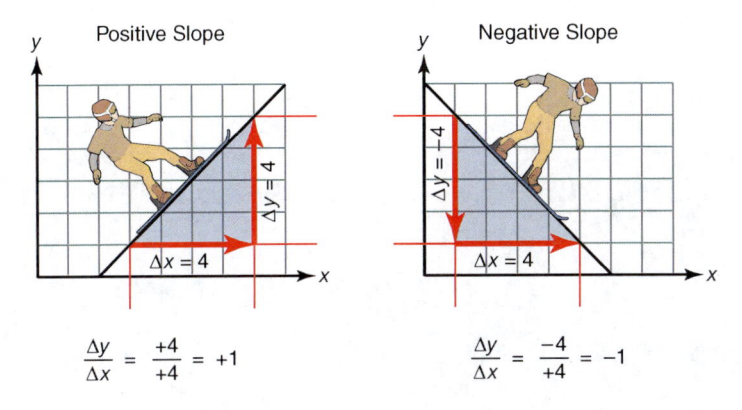

Now try calculating some slopes on your own. Start with positive slopes. Count the number of units up to find Δy. Count the number of units right to find Δx.

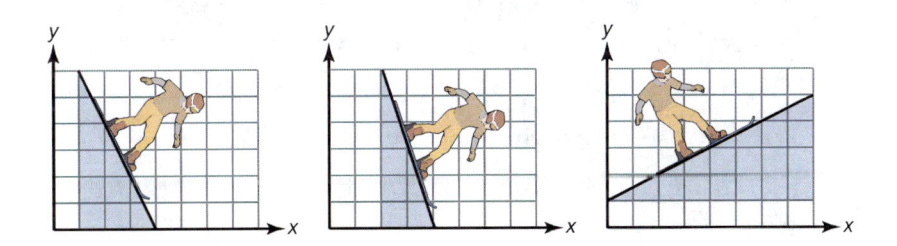

VOCABULARY

differentiate (dif uhr EN shee ayt) *v.* show how things are different

obtain (uhb TAYN) *v.* get something that you want, especially through your own effort, skill, or work

Now try figuring out some negative slopes. Count the number of units down and right. Are you beginning to notice a pattern?

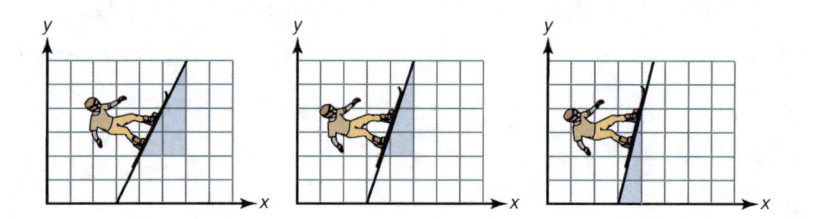

Which are the steepest positive slopes? Which are the steepest negative slopes? Can you tell how steep a slope is from the **distinctness** of its number value? Yes, you can!

Gravity and Speed

Now that you've learned about slope, let's ask the next most **logical** question. What would be the fastest kind of slope to go down? If you said a slope of -2 or -3, you'd be correct! In fact, any slope of -1 or steeper is considered "huge" in the downhill world.

This brings us to a very basic question. Why is it that the steeper the slope, the faster you go? Or put another way, what moves an object down an incline in the first place?

The short answer to this question is gravity. *Gravity* is the force that moves an object downhill. A *force* is "a push or a pull on an object." Gravity is a special kind of force because it **interacts** at a distance. For example, when you drop an egg, Earth's gravity pulls it down without touching or making **contact** with it.

The force of gravity attracts all objects toward one another. This force is weak unless one or both of the objects is huge. For example, you don't feel the force of gravity pulling you toward a tree or another person. You do, however, feel gravity pulling you toward Earth. That's because Earth is so enormous.

Vocabulary

distinctness (di STINGKT nuhs) *n.* clarity; awareness of detail
logical (LAHJ i kuhl) *adj.* reasonable; sensible
interact (in tuhr AKT) *v.* deal with or work with someone or something
contact (KAHN takt) *n.* touching; communication

Earth's gravity pulls this skateboarder downhill.

63

To understand gravity's effects, imagine a skateboarder has dropped from the edge of a cliff straight down. How fast would this free-falling skateboarder go?

To find out, you need to understand a second thing about forces. A force doesn't just put an object in motion. A force accelerates the object. *Accelerate* means to gain speed. To reduce the speed of something is to *decelerate.*

On Earth, gravity accelerates objects downward at a rate of 9.8 meters per second *each* second. This means that each second, the free-falling skateboarder increases his speed by about 10 meters per second (m/s).

We can use the acceleration of gravity to calculate the free-falling skateboarder's speed as he drops. At time 0 seconds, the skateboarder starts out at a speed of zero. At the end of each second that gravity acts on him, he gains about 10 m/s in speed.

From the table, you can **verify** how gravity accelerates an object. For example, after 5 seconds, a free-falling object's speed is 50 m/s. In more familiar terms, 50 m/s translates to over 112 miles per hour (180 km/hr).

Time (sec)	Final Speed (m/s)	Final Speed (mph)
0	0 m/s	0 mph
1	10 m/s	22 mph
2	20 m/s	45 mph
3	30 m/s	67 mph
4	40 m/s	89 mph
5	50 m/s	112 mph

Now, an interesting question arises. Will a free-falling object's speed keep increasing forever? The answer is yes. As long as some other **external** force doesn't act on it, the object will keep accelerating. However, there *is* a force that acts on falling objects. That force is air resistance. As things fall, the air pushes up at them. You see this effect when you drop a sheet of paper. The paper is so light in weight that the air really slows down, or decelerates, its fall.

Without the force of air, all objects would fall at the exact same rate. That means there would be little **distinction** between a falling sheet of paper and a falling skateboarder. If dropped from the same height, both would reach bottom at exactly the same instant.

Gravity and Distance

How far would this free-falling paper or skateboarder drop each second? If the object starts at rest, the following equation gives the distance a falling object travels.

distance = ½ gravity force • (seconds)²

We can abbreviate the equation as follows (t = time).

$d = ½ g • t^2$

Vocabulary

verify (VER uh fy) *v.* prove to be true

external (eks TER nuhl) *adj.* coming from outside something

distinctions (di STINGK shuhnz) *n.* the noting of differences between things

Since g is about 10, we can calculate each distance on the diagram.

$d = ½ (10) • (1)^2 = 5$ meters (after 1 second)

$d = ½ (10) • (2)^2 = 20$ meters (after 2 seconds)

$d = ½ (10) • (3)^2 = 45$ meters (after 3 seconds)

Now, use the equation to figure out how far the skateboarder will drop after 4 seconds. After 6 seconds. After 7 seconds. What pattern do you see?

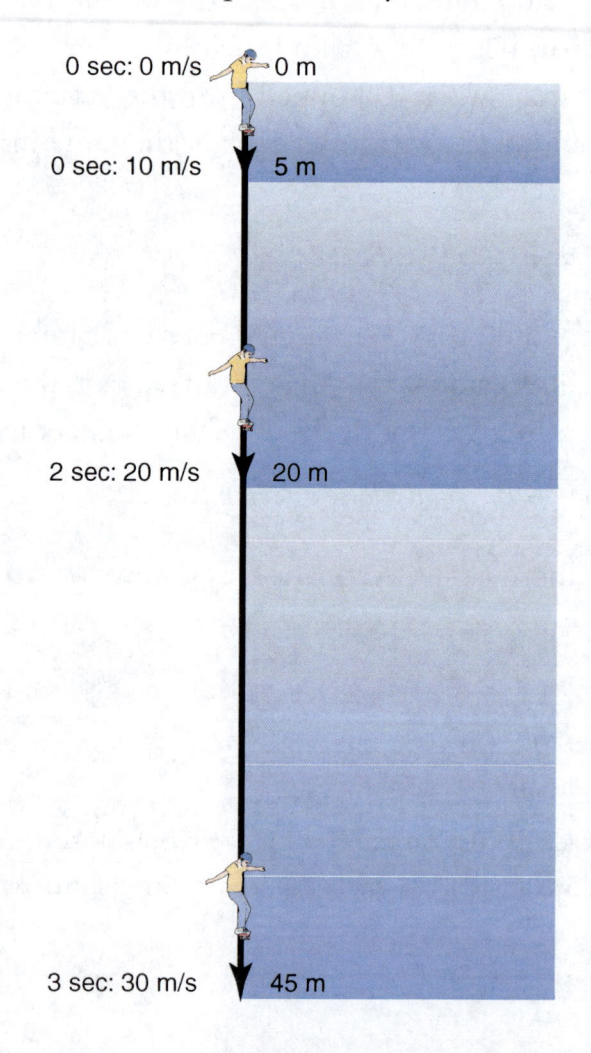

0 sec: 0 m/s — 0 m

0 sec: 10 m/s — 5 m

2 sec: 20 m/s — 20 m

3 sec: 30 m/s — 45 m

Slope and Force

Now you can see that gravity is the force that causes downhill objects to **attain** high speeds. But this explanation still doesn't answer the original question. Why do you go faster on a steep slope than on a gentle slope?

To understand what is happening, imagine a snowboarder on a flat surface with a slope of zero. Without a force pushing or pulling her, she just stands still. She doesn't move.

But now you might say, there *is* a force acting on this standing snowboarder: Gravity. It's true. Gravity does pull on the snowboarder to the same extent whether she's standing or free-falling.

So why doesn't she move? The force of gravity pulls down on her. But an equally strong force is pushing up. That force comes from the ground. The ground pushes back against gravity. In the diagram, the red arrow shows the force of gravity pulling down. The blue arrow shows the ground pushing up. The result is that the two forces cancel each other out. The net force is zero. Without the imbalance of forces acting on the snowboarder, she doesn't move.

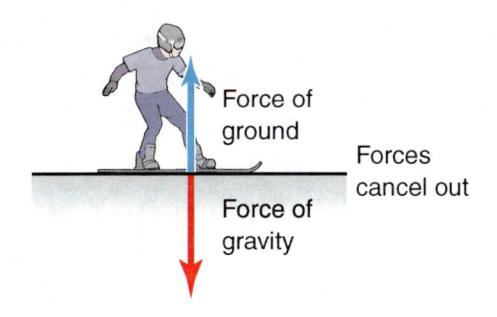

VOCABULARY

attain (uh TAYN) *v.* gain through effort; accomplish; achieve

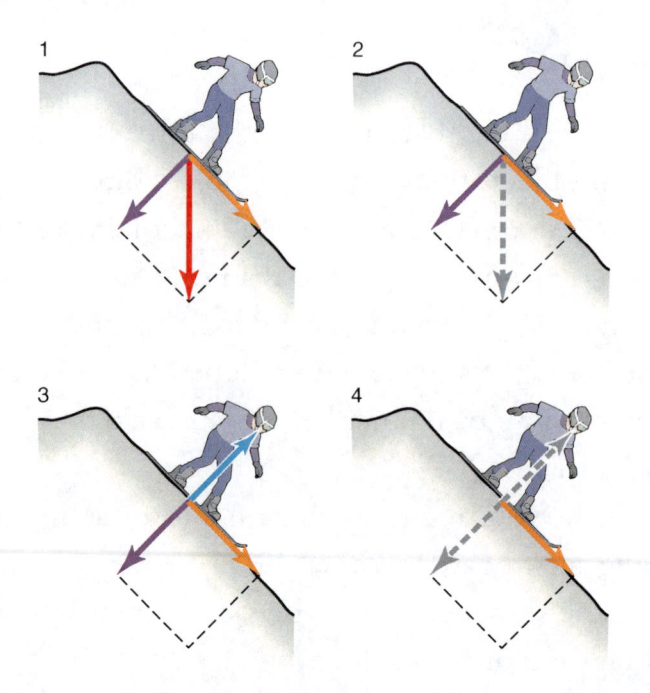

Now consider the same snowboarder going down a slope (diagram 1). Gravity, shown by the red arrow, still pulls straight down. However, on a slope, the full effect of gravity gets reduced. Diagram 2 illustrates why this effect occurs. The downward force of gravity is broken down into two perpendicular "mini-forces," shown by the purple and orange arrows.

The force that pushes straight into the hill is shown by the purple arrow in diagram 3. The force of the ground pushing back up is shown by the blue arrow. The result is that these two forces completely cancel each other out. As shown in diagram 4, only one "mini-force" remains. That force is the part of gravity that slides the snowboarder down and to the right. So the snowboarder speeds down the slope!

Back and Forth, Up and Down

Back and forth the snowboarder goes, up and down the half-pipe. It seems as if she could keep going forever. Is this possible?

Many people have wondered about questions like this, including the famous 17th-century scientist, Galileo. Galileo rolled balls up and down inclines to learn about motion and gravity. He found that a ball rolled down one side of an incline would always come back up the other side, but not quite to its initial height.

Why didn't the ball ever attain its initial height on the other side? The obvious answer is that the ball had slowed down. But what caused this slowdown?

Until Galileo, people said moving objects simply slowed down "on their own" after a while. Galileo, however, had a very different idea. He claimed that objects moving at a constant **velocity** never slow down—or change speed at all—unless some force affects them. *Velocity* is another word for *speed* but it includes direction.

A portrait of Galileo Galilei

Vocabulary

velocity (vuh LAH si tee) *n.* quantity that specifies both the speed and direction of motion of an object

In the case of the rolling ball, the force that slowed it down was **friction**. Friction is the invisible force that slows things down when they rub against each other. Friction is everywhere. You feel friction when you scrape your shoes on a sidewalk. The heat from friction makes your hands feel warm when you rub them together.

You can never completely eliminate friction. You can, however, reduce it by making a surface slick and smooth. Galileo imagined an incline that had no friction at all. In this fantasy, the initial and final height of the ball would be equal. The ball would keep rolling back and forth—and never stop!

Like Galileo, we can imagine what would happen if a snowboarder went down an incline that has no friction. Once she reached a constant velocity, the snowboarder would neither speed up nor slow down. She would just keep going forever. Her velocity would change only if some new outside force pushed her in a new direction.

Muscle Power and Momentum

As just described, friction is pretty much impossible to avoid in the real world. A smooth, slippery surface can **minimize** friction. However, even on a slick ice rink, there is friction.

This fact brings up an interesting question. Since an ice rink *does* have friction, can the skater keep gliding along without friction dragging her to a halt? Is some unseen force pushing her forward?

Speed skater Bonnie Blair is shown competing at the 1988 Olympic Winter Games in Calgary, Alberta, Canada.

Vocabulary

friction (FRIK shuhn) *n.* force that slows motion of an object when it touches another object

minimize (MIN uh myz) *v.* make the degree or amount of something as small as possible

71

Absolutely! That force comes from her own **internal** muscle power. As the skater moves, her legs push against the surface of the ice. A single push creates momentum. *Momentum* is related to force. *Momentum* is defined as "the force that keeps a moving object moving." An object with a lot of momentum is hard to slow down or stop. An object with little momentum is easier to slow down or stop.

You can calculate momentum by multiplying an object's mass, or weight, by its velocity. How much momentum does a 60-kilogram skater have moving at a speed of 3 m/s? Just multiply 60 by 3 to get momentum.

Look out! Skater B is now headed toward Skater A! Skater B weighs less than Skater A—only 40 kilograms. But Skater B is moving faster, at 5 m/s. What will happen if they collide? Will the heavier Skater A push Skater B to the right? Or will the faster Skater B push Skater A to the left?

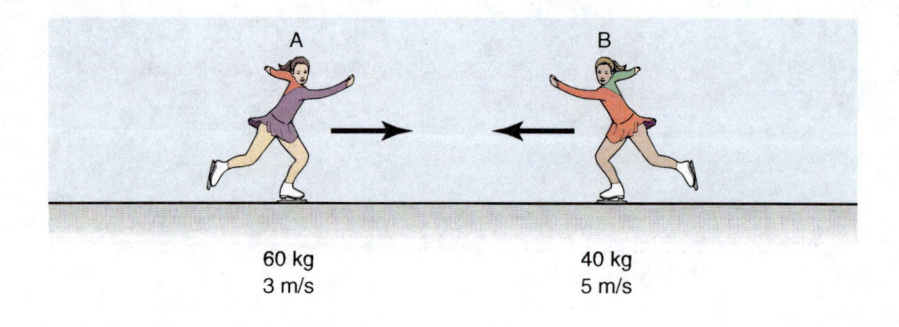

A
B
60 kg
3 m/s
40 kg
5 m/s

To find out, compare the momentum of each skater. You already saw how to find momentum by multiplying mass by velocity. So each skater's momentum would be the following:

Skater A: momentum = mass x velocity
= 60 x 3 = 180

Skater B: momentum = mass x velocity
= 40 x 5 = 200

You can see that Skater B's momentum is greater. So if the two were to collide, they would both move to the left.

Is it possible that two skaters could collide and not move right or left after the impact? Yes, if the momentum of each skater is the same. Picture this: Skater C, at 60 kilograms, is moving in one direction at 4 m/s. In the other direction, Skater D, at 30 kilograms, is moving at 8 m/s. What happens when they crash? Compute the momentum of each skater to find out—

Skater C: momentum = 60 x 4 = 240

Skater D: momentum = 30 x 8 = 240

The two skaters have the same momentum, and each is going in an opposite direction. What happens when they collide? They stop!

Vocabulary

internal (in TER nuhl) *adj.* inside something, rather than outside

The China Railway bullet train can travel at 250 km/h, but still has to deal with friction.

A World of Force and Motion

In our world, motion depends on opposing forces and actions. Why does a snowboarder speed down the slope of a half-pipe? The force of gravity pushes her. Why doesn't she move on flat ground? The downward push of gravity is opposed by the upward force of the ground.

Every motion is the result of some force or combination of opposing forces. A free-falling snowboarder moves faster than a snowboarder going down a slope. Why? The free-falling snowboarder feels the full effect of gravity. The downhill snowboarder is slowed somewhat by the upward push from the ground.

In a similar way, opposing forces also determine what happens when moving things collide. In a collision, momentum—which is related to force—plays a key role.

Which object will push the other object backward? The object that has greater momentum! So, next time you snowboard, skate, or crash into something, you know that force will be with you.

Discussion Questions

1. What are the opposing forces that affect the rate of speed of a downhill skier? Explain what happens.

2. Which opposing forces determine what happens when two moving objects collide? Explain what happens.

3. Work on your own or with a partner to solve these math problems:

    a. An object dropped from a blimp drops for 6 seconds. Ignoring the effects of air resistance, how fast is the object moving? How far has it traveled? [Answer: 60 m/s, 180 m]

    b. Skaters X and Y are heading toward each other. Skater X has a mass of 45 kilograms and travels east at 6 kilometers per hour. Skater Y has a 60-kilogram mass and moves west at 4.5 kilometers per hour. What will the result of their collision be? [Answer: both stop]

Answer Key:
Page 60: Answer: 1-C (no slope), 2-A (negative, steep), 3-E (positive, steep), 4-B (negative, moderate), 5-D (positive, moderate)

Page 62: +4 is the steepest positive slope. -4 is steepest negative slope; The higher the number, the steeper the slope, whether positive or negative.

Page 66: 4 seconds: 80 m; 6 seconds: 180 m; 7 seconds: 295 m. Pattern: the difference between distances increases by 10 for each second: 5, 15, 25, 35, 45, 55

Glossary

acquire (uh KWYR) *v.* buy or obtain something; learn or develop knowledge or skills, by your own efforts 44

acute (uh KYOOT) *adj.* sensitive; sharp 19

adapt (uh DAPT) *v.* change something so that it can be used in a different way or for a different purpose 49

affluence (AF loo uhns) *n.* wealth; abundance 15

aggravate (AG ruh vayt) *v.* make someone angry or annoyed 19

aggression (uh GRESH uhn) *n.* angry or threatening behavior or feelings that often result in fighting 15

analyze (AN uh lyz) *v.* examine or think about something carefully in order to understand it 36, 42

appreciate (uh PREE shee ayt) *v.* recognize and be grateful for; think well of; understand and enjoy 50

approach (uh PROHCH) *v.* come near or nearer to 18, 26, 44

aspect (AS pekt) *n.* the specific part that you are observing or studying 8, 27

assume (uh SOOM) *v.* think that something is true, although you have no proof of it 6

attain (uh TAYN) *v.* gain through effort; accomplish; achieve 67

ceased (SEEST) *v.* stopped 7, 28

change (CHAYNJ) *v.* become different; make someone or something become different 25

communicate (kuh MYOO ni kayt) *v.* express your thoughts and feelings clearly, so that other people understand them 46

compassion (kuhm PASH uhn) *n.* strong feeling of sympathy for people who are suffering, and a desire to help them 33

conclude (kuhn KLOOD) *v.* decide by reasoning 37, 47

consequently (KAHN si kwent lee) *adv.* as a result 9, 30

contact (KAHN takt) *n.* touching; communication 63

conviction (kuhn VIK shuhn) *n.* strong belief; certainty 8, 46

GLOSSARY

cooperate (koh AHP uhr ayt) *v.* act or work together with another or others for a common purpose **23, 46**

defeat (dee FEET) *n.* the loss of a battle, game, or race **5**

degrading (dee GRAYD ing) *adj.* insulting; dishonorable **18**

derision (di RIZH uhn) *n.* contempt; ridicule **18, 46**

dexterity (deks TER uh tee) *n.* skill using the hands or body **58**

differences (DIF uhr uhns ez) *n.* dispute; quarrel **39**

differentiate (dif uhr EN shee ayt) *v.* show how things are different **60**

distinctions (di STINGK shuhnz) *n.* the noting of differences between things **10, 50, 65**

distinctness (di STINGKT nuhs) *n.* clarity; awareness of detail **62**

disturb (di STERB) *v.* make someone feel worried or upset **31**

dominate (DAHM uh nayt) *v.* rule or control by superior power or influence **17, 45**

earn (ERN) *v.* get or deserve as a result of something you have done **37**

emphasize (EM fuh syz) *v.* show that an opinion, idea, or quality is especially important; say a word or phrase louder or higher than others to give it more importance **38, 42**

enhance (en HANS) *v.* improve the quality or condition of **46**

enrich (en RICH) *v.* improve the quality of something, especially by adding things to it **50**

evidence (EV uh duhns) *n.* facts that serve as clues or proof **36**

evidently (ev uh DENT lee) *adv.* obviously; clearly **15, 33**

examine (eg ZAM uhn) *v.* study carefully **36, 44**

expand (ek SPAHND) *v.* become large in size, number, or amount; make something become larger **27, 45**

external (eks TER nuhl) *adj.* coming from outside something **65**

77

focus (FOH kuhs) *v.* concentrate on one object or idea 42

force (FOHRS) *n.* a push or pull on an object 58

force (FOHRS) *v.* make someone do something they do not want to do 10

friction (FRIK shuhn) *n.* disagreement or angry feelings between people; force that slows motion of an object when it touches another object 18, 70

identify (eye DEN tuh fy) *v.* recognize and correctly name someone or something 44

incredulously (in KREJ oo luhs lee) *adv.* with doubt or disbelief 10

indicate (IN di kayt) *v.* show; hint at 29

infer (in FER) *v.* draw conclusions based on facts 38

interact (in tuhr AKT) *v.* deal with or work with someone or something 62

internal (in TER nuhl) *adj.* inside something, rather than outside 72

interpret (in TUR pruht) *v.* explain the meaning of; have or show one's own understanding of the meaning of 8, 57

isolate (EYE suh LAYT) *v.* set apart from others; place alone 45

logical (LAHJ i kuhl) *adj.* reasonable; sensible 62

maximize (MAK suh myz) *v.* increase something as much as possible 26

mediate (MEE dee ayt) *v.* try to help two people, groups, or countries stop arguing and make an agreement 7

minimize (MIN uh myz) *v.* make the degree or amount of something as small as possible 70

negotiation (ni goh shee AY shuhn) *n.* official discussions between two or more groups or individuals who are trying to agree on something 19 obscure (ub SKYOOR) *v.* conceal or hide **26**

obtain (uhb TAYN) *v.* get something that you want, especially through your own effort, skill, or work **60**

participate (pahr TIS uh payt) *v.* take part in an activity or event **45**

perceive (puhr SEEV) *v.* grasp mentally; make note of; observe **11, 31, 50**

presentable (pree ZENT uh buhl) *adj.* in proper order for being seen or met by others **12**

refute (ri FYOOT) *v.* give evidence to prove an argument or statement false **19, 39**

rely (ree LY) *v.* trust someone or something to do what you need or expect them to do **33**

renounced (ri NOWNSD) *v.* gave up **21**

resolute (rez uh LOOT) *adj.* determined; resolved **10**

respectively (ri SPEK tiv lee) *adv.* in the order previously named **51**

respond (ri SPAHND) *v.* react to something that has been said or done **10, 33**

select (suh LEKT) *v.* choose something or someone by carefully thinking about which is the best or most appropriate **47**

similar (SIM uh luhr) *adj.* alike **44**

simultaneously (sy muhl TAY nee uhs lee) *adv.* at the same time **12**

suffering (SUH fur ing) *n.* experiencing physical pain or distress **33**

unique (yoo NEEK) *adj.* the characteristics that make one thing different from others **16**

velocity (vuh LAH si tee) *n.* quantity that specifies both the speed and direction of motion of an object **69**

verify (VER uh fy) *v.* prove to be true **64**

victory (VIK tuhr ee) *n.* the success you achieve by winning a battle, game, or race **5**

Photo Credits

Cover: © Getty Images; **iii: t.** © Jeremy Horner/Corbis; **iii: b.** © DON EMMERT/AFP/Getty Images; **4–5:** © General Stonewall Jackson at the First Battle of Bull Run, 17th August, 1861 (colour litho) by Henry Alexander Ogden (1856-1936) (after) © Private Collection/Ken Welsh/The Bridgeman Art Library; **6–7:** © Bettmann/CORBIS; **9:** © Medford Historical Society Collection/CORBIS; **10–11:** © Bettmann/CORBIS; **12–13:** © CORBIS; **13:** inset © Hulton Archive/Stringer/Getty Images; **16–17:** © Hulton Archive/Getty Images; **18–19:** © Hulton Archive/Getty Images; **20–21:** © CORBIS; **22–23: bkgrd.** © AFP/Stringer/Getty Images; **22–23: b.** © Jeremy Horner/Corbis; **24–25:** © Dimas Ardian/Stringer/Getty Images; **24–25:** inset © AP Photo/Dita Alangkara; **28–29:** © Sally Bensusen/Photo Researchers, Inc.; **30–31:** © The Art Archive/Claude Debussy Centre St Germain en Laye/Dagli Orti; **32–33:** © CORBIS; **34–35:** © DIGITAL GLOBE/HANDOUT/epa/Corbis; **36–37:** © Marco Garcia/Stringer/Getty Images; **38:** © The Art Archive/Victoria and Albert Museum London/Sally Chappell; **38–39: bkgrd.** © AP Photo/Fadlan Arman Syam; **40–41:** © Simon Marcus/Corbis; **41:** © Hulton Archive/Getty Images; **43:** © JACKIE GLEASON ENTERTAINMENT/THE KOBAL COLLECTION; **47 and 48:** © CBS-TV/THE KOBAL COLLECTION; **50:** © NBC-TV/THE KOBAL COLLECTION; **52:** © 20TH CENTURY FOX/THE KOBAL COLLECTION; **55:** © WARNER BROS TV/BRIGHT/KAUFFMAN/CRANE PRO/THE KOBAL COLLECTION; **56:** © NBC TV/THE KOBAL COLLECTION; **58–59:** © DON EMMERT/AFP/Getty Images; **60:** © fStop/SuperStock; **63:** © Tony Freeman/Photo Edit; **69:** © Scala/Art Resource, NY; **71:** © Paul J Sutton/Duomo/Corbis; **74–75:** © AP Photo/Color China Photo